Time Spent Floating In Space

Colin R. Oldham

Made with ❤ on the BookLeaf Publishing Platform
www.bookleafpub.in
www.bookleafpub.com

Dedication

To my big sister, Maria, for always believing in me. And for pulling me back in when I float too far away.

Preface

I'm originally from Prescott, Arizona. I graduated
from Canyon View Preparatory Academy and went on to
study education and theatre at Northern Arizona
University. My time at college has opened my eyes to the
world around me, intellectually and emotionally. I don't
think I can ever go back now. This new perspective has
definitely bled into my poetry. It has bled into my beliefs.

My poetry will always be for those who are open-
minded enough to read it. I no longer want to hide
anything from anyone. To me, poetry is about letting it
all go. Ever since I started my blog, Living In A Curious
World, I've been trying to keep the rattling thoughts out
of my head and onto paper. So far it has worked. Now, I
hope this book guides my future readers to some peace
they've been seeking. Maybe not in solid answers, but in
the comfort that we're all human.

Sincerely,
    your poet,
    Colin R. Oldham

P.S. Sorry if these poems are hard to swallow. I hope
you enjoy!

Acknowledgements

Thank you to my family and friends, and most definitely my girlfriend. Thank you to my teachers from over the years that have pushed me to do better, and to all of them that saw some value in what I have to say. Thank you to all of you that have ever read my poetry! And for those that will continue to read it! At last, thank you to BookLeaf Publishing! This Writing Challenge and book have been a dream!

Aliens Drink Lemonade Just Like Us

Aliens drink lemonade just like us,
They bathe with frigid water
In the heat of the summer morning
And turn the TV on to watch armored men
Tackle each other across a hundred yards.

They get nervous before their first date,
Trying to find flowers with the most petals,
Pits sweating pulling into the long driveway.

They slam the door to capture their parents
Attention when they've been fighting all day,
And aliens miss how childhood used to taste.

They even have a hard time getting out of bed
After a night drinking with people they don't know,
And having unprotected sex with someone they'll never
see again.

And they fall into a day-to-day rhythm
Praying to a God who doesn't exist,
Hoping their life will turn around in a split second.

I even bet that aliens made it their mission
To come find us out here stranded
Because we both hate the feeling
Of being alone with too much to say.

I hope these other creatures
Learned to love before hate.
The last thing I'd want is for them to get scared away,
By 4th of July firecrackers and grinding trains.

These beings, these extraterrestrials,
These little men who come from afar,
They probably wonder how different
And how alike we are.

But the one thing I am sure of
Is when the closest star shines too hard,
Aliens drink lemonade just like us.
Topped by crushed ice and a silly straw.

I Don't Believe In Star Signs

Frankly, I don't believe in star signs
as I've been told not to,
as I've been told they're false,
as I've heard them be called pseudo.

Though it doesn't change the fact
believing in star signs is looking to the universe,
and the universe is then kind enough to talk back
which is, in my opinion,
the most beautiful form of romance.

Like Jupiter held out its hand,
and asked me for a dance.

Like Saturn got down on one knee,
and offered me one of its rings.

Like the Sun dimmed its blinding light,
for the first time, so I could look into its eyes.

Like millions and millions and millions of lightyears
away,
a giant orb of infinitely complicated matter looked at a
calendar,

and did everything in its power, to make me feel like I
was special,
because that day was my birthday; because I was born
from the stars.

Look Up Said The Tortured Father

He challenged me to trip,
From not looking down.
"You're forgetting your place"
Just look up.
enjoy the view

"Isn't it much more beautiful my boy,
After you can't see the ground?"

I think my father always wanted more
Out of the story he was born into.
I think he cried when he was old enough
To realize he couldn't fly.

I'm sure he's much happier in death,
That the space between his toes
Can no longer fill with the grainy feel of sand.

My mother always said my father
was born centuries too early.
A time where falling in space
Would be no less than normal.

Much as a kid,
It was always hard to meet his eyes.
I looked at him in awe,
By the courage it took
Every night to stare at the stars.

So, I keep looking,
I keep tripping over broken branches.
Trying to convince myself the view
Was more important than his children.

Because he loved me, I know.
Even if he was never there
To watch me grow.

Marriage

If marriage was simple then I wouldn't be here
My mom would've made the hard choice
And my dad would be out of the picture

But marriage for most is a lazy day at the river
Floating past the rose bushes at half past seven

Don't pass it on, my dad let the current take him
Floating on past the raft we paddled together

And it's happening again
It's happening again
Please don't tell me it's happening again

Because just wait one second,
I'm almost moved out
Then I give yall permission to test your limits

I'm almost to that point where life seems more steady
If I didn't, I never would've given out that promise ring

And I can tell you now,
If marriage ain't simple, it's scary

It's scary seeing your life laid out for you
Looking at someone and asking "You sure you want all
of this?"

I've become used to wrecked plans and plot twists,
Want me to tell you how to raise a depressed kid?
Come on in, I'm a seasoned veteran

Because if marriage was simple,
My parents would be seasoned veterans

Some nights I'm still sleepless
Realizing why I'd pray so much
To a god I was raised to believe in

It was because marriage is complicated
And they were just kids
No older than I am

I made a promise
Even if it doesn't fit the way I wanted it,
And I didn't make it as a kid
I slid that ring on with the most grownup, mature,
openminded, forgiving, persistent passion I could
manage

So cross my heart and hope to die
I won't be my parents

Till Death Tries To Take My Hand

Death sounds so peaceful
But I want to go through the chaos
With you, before and after the aisle

As there's a possibility
I could rest without anxiety
Until eternity eats away at my flesh
And the bugs itching away at my coffin
Become my only dear friends,
While every worry I ever mulled over
Flies out on the wind of my last breath,
Taking with it the rose bush memories
Of thorns that hurt me till the end.

What a relief that'd be
To not have to think,

Though to be honest I'd rather be,
Saving up money to buy you a ring

And wake up every single morning
To see the smile on your face,
Infusing the day with a new kind of energy.

I'd rather soak up the little free time I have
Imagining what our life might look like,
Then be able to experience it firsthand.
And realize I'm crying as you walk closer
Adorned in a lacy dress I never saw
That according to you, fits more perfect
Than the high flying few days before.

I know it's time to start my life
And the whole ceremony goes by
As I look at you and don't even notice
Everyone cheering while I kiss you
And keep going. And keep going.
Otherwise known as yours is yet again
How my destiny is and how I want it to be.
Our first meeting unlocked that sixth feeling
Unfogging the window, clearing my vision.
Because life started to make more sense
When I learned of your existence.

So yes, I'll tell you most candidly
That once I was severely depressed
And the idea of death was better than all the rest.

However, it is no longer the case,
Because when I look to my future
I can see that day,

And every day before and after that
Becomes much less gray.

Even after what feels like so little time together,
I cross my fingers and toes and everything I have
That you'll hold me tight till death tries to take my hand
Because now I know for damn sure, I won't easily give
in.

Naked

13

I've seen you naked
Only dressed in sundown's mess
And I've seen you dead

When The Clock Batteries Die For The Third Time

I can no longer handle how long the days are
Stuck in the cycle of breathing in
and wishing time would move faster
Praying to my chirping pocket guide Jiminy Cricket
that this annoying, tenuous, status quo can be shattered
Like when every wrinkled sack of bones gets pissed if
those detested turning limbs come to a screeching halt
Cause they can't handle days who stop their climb
when the clock batteries die
for the third time, they wanna go

I've honestly been confused for a while now
on how we ultimately want the gentle slap of tomorrow,
But are unprepared when the next day means jumping
from ukiyo
because the floating world rarely ever sees our love
Then comes the touch of the little boy who caresses each
flower
that ravishingly ropes our hand back into earth's sweaty
glove

(Trust me, the batteries never die)
(they live but like to watch us lie)

Once long ago I died inside
for the first and second time
I experienced the static clock twice
as the gears of my life turned quiet

I met the patient clocksmith myself
moving out of mom's
not next to packed boxes
but in the backseat on the way home
smirking when she called crying
but I never picked up the phone

I met him on another instance
about 40 more years into life
while the heavy and guilty
 beating of my heart settled
as the sun's rise, did so
to never again reach that height

When the clock batteries do die for the third time
I'll be with shut eyes, still ashamed that I had no say
I'll be waiting with sore fingers locked around double A's
shivering, whispering to myself, I don't want to go
but I know, the screw holding down the trapdoor
has always been rusted for us all.

Over Waiting

Dear one and only,
If you ever come back home
Just know I left too

While Your Head Lays Against The Window

I'm an avid believer that everything happens for a reason, that the road runs in a certain direction so every intersection is worth it in the end, but even then, I can't help the urge to pull over when it gets hard, blasting the radio, trying to block out the thoughts telling me to stop the car.

I love that you put your hands at 10&2
when mine get tired holding the wheel.
Baby, you're so beautiful sitting next to me
as we drive 95 on the freeway.
Even after 150,000 miles,
you still press my sleeping foot to the pedal.
You don't even know. You don't even know.
My sweet selfless passenger.

Tonight I'm planning to deceive you,
While you're sleeping against the window.
Again, I appreciate the lengths you've gone through
But you don't even know. I've been waiting
To pull out the rusted key which imprisons me.

I've run out of CDs, run out of games to play,
Run out of all the funny childhood stories that I know.
Sooner or later, I'll run out of gas. There's less and less
Signs letting me know how much farther I have to go.

So I'm turning off the car as an avid believer
that all roads lead home. Just at the moment
the sun stains its skies with the most breathtaking
paints.
As I pull over to kiss you on the cheek,
and hand you the note where I wrote all the best places
you never got to see. You'll wake to find the engine
asleep.

And me smiling beside you,
staring at the sun's canvas,
admiring the quiet.

Bottle Of Rum

1   See through me

    I'm a clear water ocean
    Kelp dancing on the bottom
    Stretched out grazing fish

    I'm a big bubble blown
    Out of a child's mouth
    From her party favor pouch

    I'm a safely broken mirror
    No shards not swept up
    With a face clearer than ever

    I'm everything you thought

2   I'm a bottle of rum
    Even if I say I'm not,
    "I'm not someone who gets addicted"
    You know from my eyes I'm desperate

    And you come home to a clear glass
    Without looking, know I'm done with it

And on the outside, I act fine
But internally, you know I'm burning

Torn between making me hate myself
By the reminder of how I've gone too far,
Or letting my soul give into it more

3 There's more to life than wishing it to end
You said as you left, closing the curtain

Nurses pretended to not meet my eyes
Possibly out of pity or pure embarrassment
Just speaking to say sorry when piercing my skin

And you didn't realize I apologized
For everything I did, under my breath

Not loud enough to call you back to my bed
But with enough power to find you in the wind
If I died right there squirming in the hospital

I'm sorry you saw through me so well ...

Ten Miles Till Empty

Pick me up when I'm most desperate / tonight or any
other / when my senses have dried rotten and stubborn /
and innocent / between 9th and 5th / where suburban
songs touch grass / and manicured lawns are always
kept / where I'll be outside holding my bag

Throw me in / open the sunroof / lean my chair back /
bed me on leather / let me stare at the stars / the smoke /
the crows / the bubbles / the star signs / the pollen / the
helicopter pilots

Play the loudest soft music / straight from the bellows of
cozy fall naps / play Stick Season /
Where'd All The Time Go / play Jersey Giant / when sad
/ meets beautiful / meets tragic

Roll down the windows / front and back / shatter the
windshield / front and back / let all of it in / the wind /
let in the leaves grazing the handle / let in the scents /
from passing houses / garlic bread & lasagna / from dead
skunks / from wet letters in mailboxes / and let in the
overused sprinklers / let in the nature

Lean over / give me a reminder / why I matter / why I
should care / why all my time spent floating in space /
was for myself / not for others / why you should miss me
/ when I'm gone

Drive on / drive on

Hear the tires wrestle over bumps / speedbumps /
potholes / and other cars speed by / uncomfortably close
/ hear the turning of engines / honks at stops / crying
babies in carseats / drunk drivers skidding on the road /
and the radio from before / hear it all

Make me feel / like I'm the driver / even though I know /
I know I'm not / I'm laying facing the stars / I'm the
passenger / but / do me a favor / make me feel / like I'm
in charge / like I'm in control / like I know where we're
going / and where we've gone / like this life is
everything I wanted / and I don't want / to give up / keep
driving until the wind picks up /
keep driving until the wind lifts up / that heavy feeling

Keep driving / until I can feel / everything /
ten miles till empty /

For All The Scary Creatures

I wish you knew what it felt like
To walk at night alone
Be able to show you freedom
You've never experienced before

Men are scary creatures
I know cause I am one
We peer and prod and feel
That your body is owned by all of us

But you close your legs
And pull up your shirt
As you can hear the vultures caw

I'm sorry my big sister,
For all the scary creatures,
I know what it's like to be one of us

Hoping

I was hoping
I'd cry then
so you could see
what you meant
to me.

I was hoping
you'd be excused
to stay
in this moment
or daydream
or heaven
where life
doesn't seem
so dark.

I was hoping
college would last
forever.

I was hoping
your car wouldn't
start.

I was hoping
three years
was enough
but it wasn't.

I was hoping
you'd forgive me
for giving up.

I was hoping
we made memories
that last longer
than our bodies.

I was hoping
I was weird enough
for you to easily
remember me.

I was hoping
we'd stay friends.

I was hoping
we could go back.

I was hoping
you don't dislike her
for taking priority.

I was hoping
the world doesn't
do you dirty
as you've only
shown me respect.

I was hoping
we'd make it.

I still am.

  Your best friend.

Never Been Happier

dear Friend,
remind me again
how you two met

you were/are dating him
and i Never even knew it
or suspected the Truth
because you were shown
the wicked hard Truth
in which that kind of love
- the love you dream about -
isn't one to be proud of

three years you say
three years?! that's amazing
and to think our friends
thought you were Lonely
because we joked so much
about the kind of way
you treat us
about the kind of way
you treat everyone

yet to know now

- you've been in Love -

you've been touched
by a fiery torch
long before i was

we were out of touch
and so blind in the wake
of your daydreams
that came to life before ours

you were/are gay

- we are happy -
thanks for the gift
of letting us know
our Brother
of letting us know
there's a Man
who loves you
More than a brother
- out there -

were you scared?
 - i'm sorry if you were -

were you scared?

cause i've Never been happier

you deserve as much as any of us
to get your no strings attached
- happily ever after -

now if i can know the whole how you two met - i'd be
ecstatic - but then again, the Whole truth has never been
my business - you found the perfect time to reveal what
you did - so if i need to wait, i'll do it again

i'll do it again

i'm happy i know as much i do
about my friend, and i'll do it again

Louisiana

Take Louisiana off the list
Of states I could teach in
As I only wish to subject students
To their own rightful choices
Regardless of how universal
We think the ten commandments

...

Isn't school a public institution
Full of other free religions
Inhabiting the minds of children
Who go home to their parents,
Grandparents and all kinds of relatives
That have created this reneging nation?

...

Wasn't the state created separate?
And what our precious four fathers intended?

...

Now the elephant is unmistakable
In a crowded room of salty councilmen
Where the snapping of peanuts shells
Bounce off the feathers of fermented eagles
And only the brave few try to wipe the grin
And crown off a convicted felon

...

Because it will start in the dirty boot
Then go to the biggest city in America;
It will start with disgusted looks
Then end with last chance riots;
It will start with the firing of educators
Then begin what people may call a war;
It will turn a dream into a nightmare
Then we'll be forced to endure much more

...

This isn't just Louisiana
It's playing favorites on a belief system
Like a scolding iron against my soul occupation,
So that it says in pyretic prejudice letters,
'Your kid's beautiful identity doesn't matter'

Here We Are

History lies in bed, trying its best
to fall asleep though here we are,
again and again and again,
shaking it to wake up
so that it may look upon us.

Years of disgraceful doings can be led
to a path of forgiveness, admit the facts
that no more is it doing us any kindness.

It is so unhuman.

Still we continue to pick up a book
which endorses mostly everything
that is wrong with the world.
Pick up a book that's been used
as an excuse to execute
many of history's sore spots
and beautiful people.
Pick up a book that claims to preach
love but instead fosters rage,
it condemns us to hate.

Stand up to face me then.

Put down the book
for a second,
and look at me
as a human.

Look at me like the dust
of a dead star that you are.
Look at me like the ape
of a long line of changing faces.
Look at me as a human.

Who has no greater place
in the universe and is terrified
of that very logical possibility.

Trust me, no one wants to be
in this position but here we are.
Living on a planet that was good enough
for us to make it. Stop blaming the gods
  because you're scared shitless.

Animals

got a sick feeling
when that dog leash gets yanked on
are we animals

She Loves Believing

She loves believing there's a place out there
   that hasn't been touched by the nastiest predators;
She loves believing that its trees haven't been marked
   with red X's, cut down to make a cabin;
She loves believing that its sands bare no footprints
   or plastic bags from every possible supermarket;
She loves believing that its wind smells sweet
   like the infant Earth, rather than 4 dollars for a gallon;
And she loves believing that no matter how alone
   the other animals might feel, they'll never
   in their wildest dreams, think of inviting humans

Because the place is perfect how it is.

Stroll

I stroll the pathway between two lawns
and step off.

There is kicked-up grass from nearby careless travelers,
swept along by my dijon high tops,
and kissed rightfully on the cheek
from neighbors blowing their best wishes.

There is trees carved into indecipherable human initials,
possibly knife cut or from the will of their heart,
and its branches bare naked for all of us to see
as we rush to our next destination.

There is bricks, and windows,
and nature mutilated.

There is rocks cemented between pavement,
slipping past my toes, resting above stripped-down soles,
and there is one in my hand, and I throw it.

There is unkept garbage cans next to more trash
where someone decided they had something better to do
than dispose of their mess.

There is bikes, all sorts of colors and sunburnt,
cramped together with some tied up, some not,
statically waiting and recovering from their last run.

And there is sun,
effortlessly reminding me the day isn't over,
racking its long, wet tendrils on my neck.

And there is beeping and whirring
and wires and cords and so many phones.

There is quiet in this quick-paced busyness
like everyone is dreaming of the later,
like even the grass and the trees and the rocks
and the trash want to go home,
like the whole entire world doesn't want to be here
    but it has to.

Anymore

I woke up late for the gym this morning but I still went.
My building's broke in half. So you have to exit into the
second week of February wind, before coming back in to
sweat. And I had to piss. I always have to piss. My
friends tell me that. The bathroom was so fluorescent, so
tiled, so white that I thought I was dead. It took me back
to when Pretty Princess wasn't doing so well. Why it
brought me back to that I don't know. She was sick for a
while. She was sick like her intestines had exploded on
the couch, and she wasn't breathing so well. She was so
frightfully pulling in air every time I opened the door
after school. I felt bad. I think we all felt bad. I think we
all felt it was better to lay her down to rest. There is no
nicer way to say that. The bathroom tiles, those white
squares like hopscotch, reminded me of the floor I sat on
while I pet her. It was cold. I was wearing shorts. But she
had a blanket to shield her paws from the hospital
weather. We huddled around her. I think we all felt no
one was entitled to simply possess her last minutes. We
were a family like that. When they brought in the
drought, I couldn't see it go in. Her fur was too thick. It
took on the many colors a dog could have, but never
stayed. Her fur is still probably in that room, and in that
house, and on my clothes. I wish I could wear something

similar to clothes where she stays. Like a shirt with her face, or name. Like a necklace with a dog tag. Because in that moment, I didn't realize how little she left. In that moment in the clinic, when she was still excited, when she was still living through pure happiness, when she was still standing and wanting to jump, when she was still looking at everyone she loved, I didn't realize I'd want to go back. And hold her again. Because when she finally settled down, eyes closed and heart slowed, she didn't look like her anymore. They took her away to an unseen fire. She didn't look like her anymore. I collapsed onto the floor in the bathroom stall, and I realized I didn't look like me anymore. It was cold. I was wearing shorts.

Hearing The End

Holding hands clapped against flashbacks
Amidst the dying light that rears its roar to the moon.
Pebbles and dirt wash down into a shower
Between moments of soft screams from nearby
headstones.
And my mother, her mother, and the mothers before her
Come up with a violent crash of whittled laughs
To memorialize the humor in my performance.

I had a great laugh.

     Did you hear it?

          It isn't here yet.